Can the Earth Survive?

Waste and Recycling Challenges

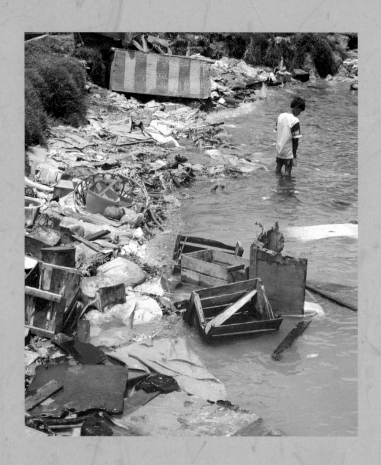

Louise Spilsbury

rosen publishing's
rosen
central

New York

Published in 2010 by The Rosen Publishing Group Inc.
29 East 21st Street, New York, NY 10010

First Edition

Commissioning editor: Jennifer Schofield
Designer: Jane Hawkins
Picture researcher: Kathy Lockley
Illustrator: Ian Thompson
Proofreader: Susie Brooks

Library of Congress Cataloging-in-Publication Data

Spilsbury, Louise.
    Waste and recycling challenges / Louise Spilsbury. — 1st ed.
        p. cm. — (Can the earth survive?)
    Includes bibliographical references and index.
    ISBN 978-1-4358-5355-3 (library binding)
    ISBN 978-1-4358-5486-4 (paperback)
    ISBN 978-1-4358-5487-1 (6-pack)
    1. Pollution—Environmental aspects—Juvenile literature. 2.
    Recycling (Waste, etc.)—Juvenile literature.   I. Title.
    TD176.S68 2010
    363.72'8—dc22

                                              2008052469

Picture Acknowledgements:
The author and publisher would like to thank the following agencies for allowing these
pictures to be reproduced: Rob Bowden/EASI-images: 16; Andrew Brown/Ecoscene: 4BL;
Adrian Cooper/EASI-images: 22; Digital Vision Ltd/Getty: Cover, 1, 10, 13, 14, 18, 20, 24, 28,
29, 39T; Mark Edwards/Still Pictures: 43; Mary Evans Picture Library: 4BR; Peter M.
Fisher/Corbis: 32; Image Source/Corbis: 6; Oldrich Karasek/Still Pictures: 39B; Catherine
Karnow/Corbis: 34; Frans Lanting/Corbis: 44; Roy Maconachie/EASI-images: 17; Will & Deni
McIntyre/Corbis: 8; NASA/Alamy: 25; RSA: 11; sinopictures/Readfoto/Chan/Still Pictures: 40;
Michael S. Yamashita/Corbis: 30. iStockphoto: 33, 35, 36

Manufactured in China

Contents

A Wasteful World

Overflowing trash cans, rivers choked with litter, beaches strewn with garbage—scenes like these are becoming more and more common around the world. Today, more waste than ever before is being produced. As well as cluttering up the environment, these mountains of waste are potential problems for the health of the planet and all of the living things on Earth.

Waste in the Past

For a long time after the first people walked the Earth, over half a million years ago, humans created little garbage. One of the reasons for this was that people wasted very little. Instead, they reused and repaired most of what they had, for example, food scraps were fed to animals that they reared for food, manure was used to enrich the soil they grew crops on, and broken tools were repaired rather than replaced. People produced some waste, such as the pieces of pottery that archaeologists have gathered as evidence of the way they lived, but the population was small, so the impact of this waste was small, too.

▲ There were clean beaches by St. Michael's Mount years ago.

◄ The same beaches are littered with plastic trash today.

Evidence

KINDS OF WASTE

There are two main types of waste: biodegradable and nonbiodegradable. Waste made from natural materials, such as food waste, is biodegradable. This means that it can be broken down by rain and animals, such as worms. It can also be digested by creatures, such as bacteria and molds, until it becomes part of the soil. This kind of waste is useful because it returns nutrients to the soil, which helps plants to grow. Much of the waste people produce today, however, is nonbiodegradable. It is made from synthetic materials that take much longer to rot.

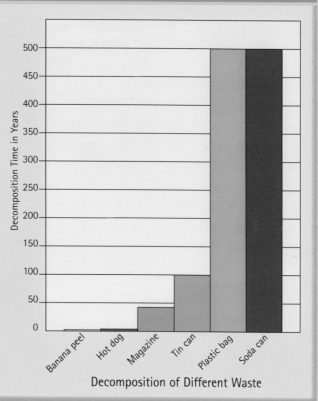

Decomposition of Different Waste

The Industrial Revolution

As populations grew, more and more waste was produced, but the real change came with the Industrial Revolution, which began in the early 1700s. *Industrialization* is the use of machines to make products and of factories to make many versions of the same thing. Industrialization meant that more goods were produced cheaply, so people could buy more. And because products were cheaper, people could afford to replace them when they broke, discarding the old items as waste. By the twentieth century, disposable items—designed to be used once or a few times and then thrown away—were invented as a way to keep people buying. Although disposables such as plastic pens and diapers are useful, they have also resulted in more waste.

Global Differences

The differences between the amount of waste produced by rich and poor people is huge. Some consumers in more economically developed countries (MEDCs) buy, eat, and use much more than other people. They also produce vast amounts of waste, much of it nonbiodegradable. In less economically developed countries (LEDCs) people do not have money to buy many things and their rates of consumption and, therefore, waste are ten or more times lower than people in MEDCs. In poorer places, people have to reuse or repair things because they cannot afford to buy them new. For example, the city of Los Angeles produces around 2,769 pounds (1,256 kilograms) of trash per person each year. People in Abidjan, on the Ivory Coast, generate only 440 pounds (200 kg) of trash a year.

Why Waste Matters

The Earth provides most of the resources that people use and later discard as waste. Resources are things that people need and use, such as wood from trees, oil from beneath the Earth's surface, and water. There is a danger that if resources are used and thrown away at the current rate, they will run out.

The waste that people produce threatens the Earth in another way. Where people put their waste and how they dispose of it is a tricky business. The waste that is buried in the ground, burned into the air, and released into rivers and the sea damages the Earth's environment. In the future, the Earth may no longer be able to cope with the amounts of waste produced, leaving the environment in serious danger.

▶ Some countries in Europe are already struggling to deal with the amount of waste people produce and overflowing trash cans may be left uncollected.

Evidence

WORLD WASTERS

This map compares the average amounts of waste produced per person per year in 2002. It shows waste collected from homes, schools, and businesses in regions around the world. It excludes wastes from industry. As you can see, areas such as Western Europe, the Middle East, and Japan produce the most waste. These are areas where most of the more economically developed countries are. Much smaller amounts of waste are generated by parts of Africa, eastern Asia, and Eastern Europe, which contain more LEDCs.

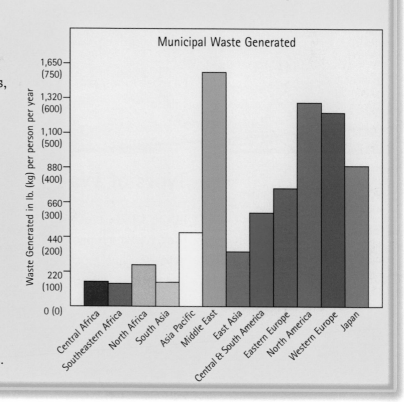

Municipal Waste Generated

Waste Generated in lb. (kg) per person per year

1,650 (750)
1,320 (600)
1,100 (500)
880 (400)
660 (300)
440 (200)
220 (100)
0 (0)

Central Africa, Southeastern Africa, North Africa, South Asia, Asia Pacific, Middle East, East Asia, Central & South America, Eastern Europe, North America, Western Europe, Japan

The Lowdown on Waste

Do you have any idea how much waste you generate in an ordinary day in your life? Almost everything people do creates waste of some kind. In an MEDC, household waste accounts for about one-tenth of the country's entire waste.

▲ School lunchboxes often contain large amounts of wasteful packaging, such as paper napkins, plastic cups and bottles, food wrappers, and juice cartons. In the U.S.A., a typical schoolchild creates just over 66 lbs. (30 kg) of school lunch packaging waste every school year.

Types of Waste

In the 1950s, most trash cans were full of ashes from coal fires, on which people burned most of their household garbage. Now most houses in MEDCs have central heating and nothing is burned at home. The trash cans people fill with waste contain pizza cartons, cans, and other food packaging, as well as piles of paper. In spite of the fact most people in MEDCs have clean water piped to their homes, their trash cans are also full of plastic water bottles as well as other plastic products. Many of these plastic products are

Evidence

WHAT'S IN YOUR CAN?

This pie chart shows the contents of an average trash can in the United Kingdom. The waste produced would differ if the household did not include a baby or had more than one baby. It would also differ if everyone in the house was out at school or work all day, but it does give an idea of the kinds of waste thrown away every day. For example, it tells us that most of the waste that people produce at home is kitchen, yard, and paper and board waste. If you add together the paper and board, glass, metal packaging, dense plastic, and plastic wrap, 35 percent of household waste, or over one-third of the waste, is from old newspapers and packaging alone.

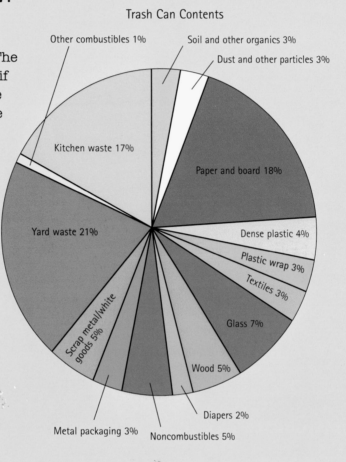

Trash Can Contents

- Other combustibles 1%
- Soil and other organics 3%
- Dust and other particles 3%
- Kitchen waste 17%
- Paper and board 18%
- Yard waste 21%
- Dense plastic 4%
- Plastic wrap 3%
- Textiles 3%
- Scrap metal/white goods 5%
- Glass 7%
- Wood 5%
- Metal packaging 3%
- Noncombustibles 5%
- Diapers 2%

treated as disposable, such as diapers and razors, but in fact, they are the opposite because they hang around in piles of waste for centuries.

Added to the packaging waste there is yard and kitchen waste, such as garden clippings and vegetable peelings. People often overstock their refrigerators, so kitchen waste may include food that has passed its use-by date. Household waste also includes things such as broken toys, worn-out toasters, and other broken appliances.

IT'S A FACT

People in MEDCs throw away about seven times their body weight in trash every year.

What is E-Waste?

Increasing numbers of everyday consumer items, from toothbrushes to teddy bears, contain electronic parts. Electronic and electrical equipment make up on average 4 percent of household and office waste in Europe, and the amount of electronic waste, or e-waste as it is known, produced is growing three times faster than any other type of waste.

▲ Growing mountains of e-waste are piling up around the globe.

What Causes E-Waste?

Some kinds of electrical and electronic equipment, including washing machines and remote-controlled toys, are thrown away when they become broken or worn out. However, many kinds of electronic goods, including computers, games consoles, and cell phones, are becoming increasingly short lived. Many electronic products are thrown away when they still work, because people want to buy newer versions with more features or models that simply look more fashionable. In the United States, about half of all the computers that are thrown away are in good, working order and although a cell phone should last about seven years, most people change them after just 11 months.

IT'S A FACT

The United Nations Environment Programme estimates that up to 50 million tons of e-waste are generated every year. Half of all these electrical goods actually work or would require only very basic repairs to make them work again.

Evidence

WHAT'S IN A COMPUTER?

By 2010, there will be 716 million new computers in use in the world. Given that the average lifespan for a computer is less than two years, it is easy to see why computer waste will be a huge issue in the future. The problem is not just the amount of plastic and metal waste that will pile up. Computers and cell phones contain poisonous chemicals and metals that cannot be disposed of safely or easily. The chemicals and metals in a computer like this one may not be a problem while the machine is in use, but they can leak out when the computer is disposed of.

Computer Parts
1: Lead in cathode ray tube and solder
2: Arsenic in older cathode ray tubes
3: Selenium in circuit boards as power supply rectifier
4: Polybrominated flame retardants in plastic casings, cables, and circuit boards
5: Antimony trioxide as flame retardant
6: Cadmium in circuit boards and semiconductors
7: Chromium in steel as corrosion protection
8: Cobalt in steel for structure and magnetivity
9: Mercury in switches and housing

The Problem With E-waste

The problem with e-waste is that it is made from a lot of different materials that cannot be reused until the product is dismantled and its different parts are separated. This is usually a very difficult and expensive process. There is also the problem of the toxic substances found in e-waste. Toxic metals such as lead, cadmium, mercury, and arsenic are used in the circuits and soldered wires of electronic equipment such as computers.

▶ This WEEE sculpture—WEEE stands for Waste Electrical and Electronic Equipment—is made from the amount of waste electrical and electronic products that an average U.K. citizen throws away in a lifetime. The WEEE man is 23 feet (7 meters) high and includes five refrigerators, 35 cell phones, five sandwich toasters, and four lawnmowers. Each tooth is made from a computer mouse!

Sewage

Sewage is another significant kind of household waste. Sewage is the waste that is flushed down the toilet and washed down the sink. In some countries, waste water runs down the drainpipe then through underground pipes, called sewers, until it reaches a sewage treatment plant. Here, the sewage flows through a variety of filters, tanks, and chemicals until it is cleaned. The cleaned water is then poured into rivers or the sea. The sludge waste that has been removed from the sewage is usually spread over land, burned, or dumped at sea.

Sewage Problems

The problem with sewage is that, in many countries, it is dumped into waterways without being treated. In fact, in LEDCs, as much as 90 percent—that is nine out of every ten gallons of waste water—is discharged without treatment into rivers, streams, and seas. As well as being unsightly and unpleasant, this raw sewage can contain harmful bacteria and viruses that cause diseases. Sometimes, in countries with sewage systems, bacteria or poisons slip through the system and find their way into the environment.

▶ When sewage and urban runoff collect in rivers and lakes, the pollution can kill fish and other water animals.

CASE STUDY
Sewage and the Great Lakes

The United States and Canada are considered to be two of the most advanced nations in the world, but raw sewage is still a problem in the five huge lakes known as the Great Lakes. The Great Lakes basin, the region around the rivers that flow into the Great Lakes, is home to more than one-tenth of the population of the U.S.A. and one-quarter of the population of Canada. Around 29 billion gallons (109 billion liters) of untreated sewage enter the Great Lakes every year through sewage overflows from cities such as Detroit and Ottowa. The problem is that these cities have increased in size and population since their sewage systems were built, and the old-fashioned systems cannot cope with the huge amounts of sewage that flow through them today. In 2006, an expert said, "We need to change our ways and stop treating the Great Lakes like a toilet."

Urban Runoff

The waste water that collects in our gutters and drains contains more than sewage. The water that washes off streets, sidewalks, and yards also carries many contaminants. These include oil, gasoline, paints, household chemicals, animal feces, metals, and litter. This waste is known as "urban runoff", because it mostly runs off the concrete surfaces of settlements where lots of people live and create waste. Sometimes these types of waste can flow directly into rivers and oceans. They may become increasingly toxic as they build up.

IT'S A FACT

Each day, the people in a large city like New York create enough sewage to fill more than 3,000 Olympic-size swimming pools.

Industrial Waste

Industrial waste is the name given to the different types of waste produced by the various manufacturing processes that take place in factories. Industrial wastes include food waste, chemical waste, fuels, oils and greases, and rubble. For example, metal ores are substances extracted from rocks to make metals. The rest of the rock is treated as waste. The construction industry creates large amounts of bulky waste, including bricks, concrete, wood, and glass when demolishing old buildings and building new ones.

Waste Gases

It takes a great deal of power to make products in factories. Most power is produced by burning coal or gases in power stations. Waste gases from this process are released into the air through giant chimneys. Waste gases, such as carbon dioxide, are also released into the air by the vehicles used to transport goods made by industries.

Agricultural Wastes

To prevent insect pests and control weeds, farmers use chemical sprays called pesticides. To help crops to grow well, they use chemical fertilizers. Some of these chemicals, such as nitrates, drain into the soil or are washed by rain into nearby rivers as waste.

Another waste produced by the agricultural industry is animal waste, or manure. Some livestock farms today are huge and contain thousands of animals, so animal waste is a big issue. For example, in the U.S.A., over 1 billion tons of animal waste are produced every year.

▶ Waste gases from industries billow into the atmosphere. Winds may blow them over a wide area.

IT'S A FACT

It has been estimated that for every ton of products bought, 10 tons of resources have been used to manufacture them.

Evidence

WHO MAKES MOST WASTE?

This pie chart shows the share of waste produced by different sectors of the U.K. population. It seems to suggest that agriculture and industry are responsible for more waste than households.

But it must be remembered that these industries are producing goods for people, so the waste they produce is really connected to household waste, too. For example, the chemical and pesticide waste produced by farmers is used to grow food, and the wood waste left over from paper making is used to make items such as magazines and school books.

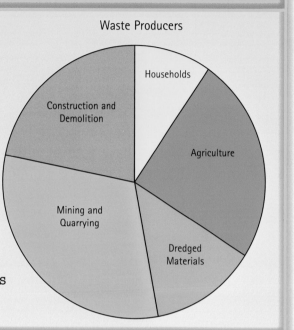

Waste Producers

- Households
- Construction and Demolition
- Agriculture
- Mining and Quarrying
- Dredged Materials

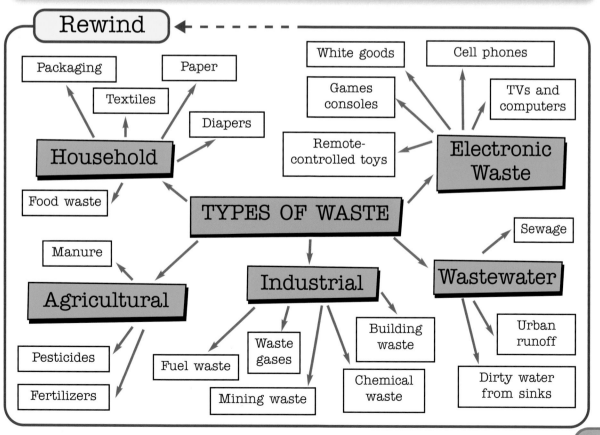

Rewind

TYPES OF WASTE

Household
- Packaging
- Paper
- Textiles
- Diapers
- Food waste

Electronic Waste
- White goods
- Cell phones
- Games consoles
- TVs and computers
- Remote-controlled toys

Agricultural
- Manure
- Pesticides
- Fertilizers

Industrial
- Fuel waste
- Waste gases
- Mining waste
- Building waste
- Chemical waste

Wastewater
- Sewage
- Urban runoff
- Dirty water from sinks

15

What Happens to Waste?

Many people never think about what happens to the waste they throw away, because after it is collected by dump trucks, they never see it again. Globally, the way waste is dealt with differs greatly. In some places, people have to deal with their waste themselves, but in others, it becomes part of a complex waste treatment system.

Dumps

In many countries, there is no such luxury as a trash collection service and in most LEDCs, there is a shortage of waste treatment systems or none at all. In many of these places, waste is piled up on areas of wasteland, or left on the roadsides in the hope that it will rot. On the outskirts of large cities in some LEDCs, mountains of waste have formed. Often, people dump waste into the sea or rivers, believing that the waste will eventually be broken down by the water.

▼ Waste is transported on barges rather than trucks in Hong Kong, China.

CASE STUDY
Garbage City

Growing piles of trash are a problem for many cities around the world, but in Cairo, Egypt, the Zabaleen people have been successfully dealing with Egypt's biggest waste mountains for 50 years. The Zabaleen are a group of people who moved from villages in Upper Egypt to Cairo. About 30,000 Zabaleen live in a quarry outside Cairo known as Garbage City. They live off the leftovers thrown out by the city's 18 million inhabitants.

Fathers and sons collect the garbage, using donkeys and carts or small trucks, for free or a small fee. Then the women in the families sort the waste into different types, including plastics, glass, metal, paper, and textiles.

The Zabaleen make money from feeding food and vegetable waste (about two-thirds of the total) to raise and sell livestock and by carefully sorting, washing, and reselling as much as they can of the rest.

Collecting and processing garbage is hard work and living among and handling so much waste means that some Zabaleen people suffer from health problems. Nevertheless, the Zabaleen provide a vital service and are proud of their record of collecting and processing about one-third of Cairo's trash.

▼ The Zabaleen people's way of life may be under threat as waste disposal companies start to take over the job of clearing Cairo's streets of trash. But will it be an improvement? Although the Zabaleen reuse almost everything they collect, the modern refuse trucks will simply crush it and pile it up.

How Landfill Sites Work

Garbage trucks collect trash and take it to landfill sites. There, a machine called a compactor, which presses the trash into layers, crushes the piles of waste. These layers are covered with soil to prevent smells and to stop the waste from attracting animal pests, such as rats and flies. When the landfill hole is completely full, the site is covered over and the land is often used again, for example, for golf courses. In the U.S.A., three of the country's main airports, including La Guardia in New York, are built on top of landfill sites.

Landfill is a cheap option and has been widely used around the world. It is also the only option for many types of waste. One of the problems with landfill, however, is that many sites are already full and some countries are running out of suitable land to create new ones, especially since no one really wants to live near one.

▼ Giant tractors spread out waste at an enormous landfill site. They have special tires to prevent them from sinking into the trash.

Incineration

In most countries, incineration is the second-largest waste disposal method. Incinerators burn waste and work like giant ovens. Gases released by burning the waste may be taken and used to generate electricity and the ash, left over at the bottom of the incinerators when waste is burned, is usually collected and put into landfill sites or mixed with other building materials to make roads or cement blocks. Even so, many people say that incinerators are a waste of waste, because the trash that they burn includes materials such as wood, glass, plastic, and metal that could all be used again in some way.

Evidence

HOW INCINERATORS WORK

Waste is dumped into the holding area (1), until it is picked up and dropped into a container called a hopper (2). The waste is then pushed into the incinerator (3) and is burned at 1,382 degrees Fahrenheit (750 degrees Celsius)—four times hotter than a domestic oven. Heat from the incinerator boils water in a boiler (4), and steam from this passes to a generator to produce electricity. Ash from the fire falls into a collection area (5), and gases from the fire pass through a machine (6) that removes some of the poisons from the gas. Tiny bits of dust are then removed from the gas (7) before it passes out through a chimney.

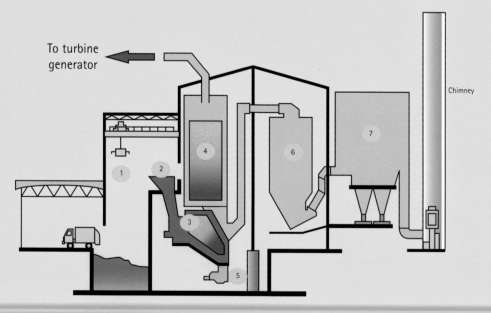

To turbine generator

Chimney

Dealing with Hazardous Waste

Hazardous waste is waste that is dangerous to treat, keep, or dispose of, because it could be harmful to human, plant, or animal life. These wastes may be explosive, catch fire easily, or release toxic fumes. Hazardous wastes can include batteries, discarded gas bottles, and computer monitors. In many countries, laws state that hazardous waste must be taken to special disposal sites. For example, harmful chemical waste may be taken from factories in secure tankers for treatment. The waste produced by nuclear power stations is hazardous and can remain so for thousands of years, so it must be disposed of very carefully. Some nuclear waste is set in concrete and stored in sealed drums and boxes that may be buried deep underground. In general, disposal of hazardous waste costs at least 36 times as much as the disposal of general waste.

▼ This U.K. dump is for the remains of treated or refined toxic waste.

CASE STUDY
Nigeria's E-Waste Mountains

The export of old computers to Nigeria began as a way of providing the country with secondhand but working computers. Unfortunately, three-quarters of the machines sent to Nigeria are beyond repair and have no value at all. The country is in danger of becoming the world's computer dumping ground, with waste computers building up in huge piles at the edge of cities and leaking potentially dangerous chemicals into Nigeria's land. As a result, the United Nations has called for an end to Western countries using Africa as a landfill for their e-waste.

Exporting Waste

Many countries have begun to export waste, usually sending it to LEDCs to be disposed of. This sometimes happens because a country is running out of its own landfill sites. Another reason countries export waste is because it is cheaper. In many cases, this is because wages for people who deal with waste are lower in LEDCs, but in the case of electronic waste, such as computer monitors or cell phones, it is because many LEDCs do not have laws as strict as those in MEDCs about the disposal of hazardous waste. LEDCS may develop specialized recycling industries but import environmental and health problems along with the waste from MEDCs.

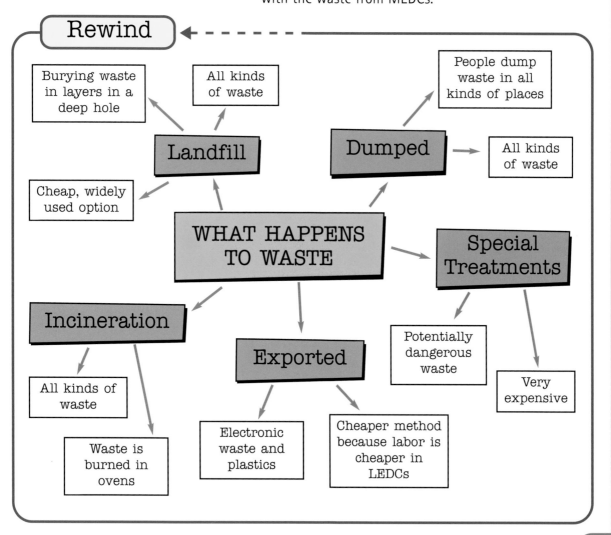

Rewind

WHAT HAPPENS TO WASTE

Landfill
- Burying waste in layers in a deep hole
- All kinds of waste
- Cheap, widely used option

Dumped
- People dump waste in all kinds of places
- All kinds of waste

Special Treatments
- Potentially dangerous waste
- Very expensive

Incineration
- All kinds of waste
- Waste is burned in ovens

Exported
- Electronic waste and plastics
- Cheaper method because labor is cheaper in LEDCs

The Impact of Waste

One of the major impacts of waste is that it creates air pollution and this has wide-reaching effects. Air pollution is a global problem—the pollution caused by waste in one part of the world can blow on the wind to affect other places far away.

▲ The World Health Organisation (WHO) says that every year, 3 million people across the globe are killed by outdoor air pollution from vehicles and industrial emissions.

Waste Disposal and Pollution

When waste in landfill sites rots, it not only produces a nasty smell, but it also releases large amounts of methane. Many incinerator chimneys release smoke containing dust, particles of metals, and gases such as carbon dioxide. Methane and carbon dioxide are greenhouse gases. They spread like a blanket in the atmosphere, trapping heat at the Earth's surface. Many scientists believe these gases are leading to the widespread increases in temperature and changing weather patterns called climate change.

Many modern incinerators clean smoke before it is released (see page 19), but most still create one-third more carbon dioxide than gas-fired power stations. This is significant, but even so this carbon dioxide is less damaging to the atmosphere than the methane gas that would be released if the waste was buried instead of burned.

Acid Rain

Acid rain is a result of air pollution caused mainly by waste gases from power stations that burn fossil fuels, such as coal and gas. Acidic gases are released from tall stack chimneys, and when they mix with droplets of water in the sky, they form acid rain. When acid rain falls to Earth, it can damage many living things: it increases the acidity of the water in lakes, killing fish and other aquatic life, and it also prevents trees and other plants from taking in the nutrients from the soil that they need to remain healthy.

Air Pollution and Health

Tiny particles of dust and waste gases in the air that are released from vehicles, factories, and waste disposal systems can have a serious effect on people's health. Some waste chemicals in the air can cause problems, from headaches to brain damage. Dust from asbestos waste can cause cancer. Air pollution also causes or worsens breathing and lung diseases, such as asthma and bronchitis. In some places, people also suffer from eye problems caused by polluted air, which can eventually lead to blindness.

Evidence

WASTE GASES IN THE ARCTIC

You might imagine that the North Pole is safe from air pollution since few people live there and so little waste is produced. However, air pollution can travel long distances. This map shows that winds that blow from North America, Asia, and Europe can carry air pollution as far as the North Pole. Particles in the waste gases settle into the water, snow, and ice there. As a result, the people and animals of the North Pole have some of the highest amounts of toxins in their bodies of any place on Earth.

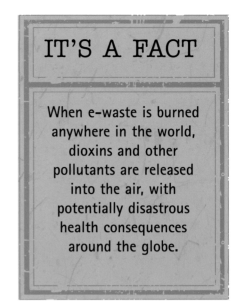

Southern Asia

North Pole

Eastern USA

Europe

Ocean Pollution

Waste gets into the world's oceans in a number of ways. Some waste, such as litter, old fishing nets and waste from ships is dumped directly into seawater. Sometimes waste gets into the sea accidentally, for example, when oil leaks from ships. In some places, factories release chemical waste straight into rivers that run into seas, and sewage is often pumped into oceans. Between 30 and 50 million tons of untreated or partially treated sewage is dumped in the Mediterranean sea every year, and over 100,000 tons of oil is dumped in the North sea by ships cleaning their tanks and dumping the dirty water overboard.

Ocean Food Chains

Ocean waters can break down most waste, but the waste does not disappear. When a marine animal swallows even a small amount of toxic waste, it is gradually passed up the food chain. In the food chain, one animal is eaten by another, larger animal, which is eaten by another animal, and so the pollutants are passed on. Because humans eat fish and other seafood, the toxins may end up in people's food. Eating contaminated seafood could harm people in various ways, including causing fever and in extreme cases, brain damage. And just like the winds that carry air pollution, ocean currents can transport pollutants all around the world, affecting food chains everywhere.

◀ This market area on the coast of Borneo is choked with rubbish dumped in the sea.

CASE STUDY
The Great Barrier Reef

The Great Barrier Reef off the coast of Australia is the world's largest coral reef system. It is made up of almost 3,000 coral reefs, which together cover an area of about 132,973 square miles (344,400 sq km). Coral reefs are made by tube-shaped animals, called coral polyps, when they form a hard mineral skeleton around themselves. This is a slow process as coral grows at a rate of about half an inch (13 mm) a year and the reef is an important habitat for many marine animals. Unfortunately, satellite images suggest that river water polluted by pesticide waste is reaching the Great Barrier Reef, where it threatens to damage this natural wonder and the marine animals that live among it.

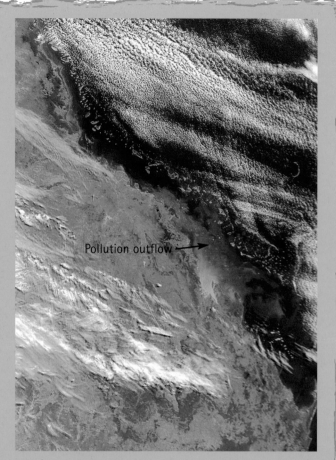

Pollution outflow ←

▲ Due to polluted river water, the Great Barrier Reef is under threat.

The Plastics Problem

Plastic poses a greater threat to marine life than any other kind of waste. There are around 13,000 pieces of plastic litter per square kilometre of the world's oceans. Some animals swallow pieces of plastic, which stick in their throats and stop them from breathing or make their stomachs feel so full that they stop eating and eventually starve to death. Some animals become tangled in plastic at sea or on coasts and they drown, or starve because they cannot fly away to find food, or become easy targets for predators.

IT'S A FACT

It is estimated that across the world over one million birds and 100,000 marine mammals and turtles die every year from becoming tangled in or swallowing plastics.

River Pollution and Wildlife

Waste in rivers affects wildlife in various ways. Animals can choke if they swallow waste or drown if they become tangled in it. For example, in the United Kingdom, about 4,000 mute swans die each year after becoming tangled in discarded fishing tackle or after swallowing the lead weights thrown away by anglers. Some chemical substances that enter freshwater streams and rivers in high concentrations can kill fish and other animals immediately. Sometimes pollutants build up until they reach dangerous levels, eventually killing birds, fish, and mammals.

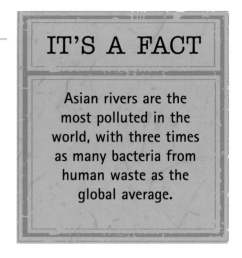

IT'S A FACT

Asian rivers are the most polluted in the world, with three times as many bacteria from human waste as the global average.

If oil gets into a slow-moving river, it forms a thin layer over the water's surface that prevents oxygen from entering the water. Without oxygen, the water cannot support plant or animal life. Rivers and lakes also become starved of oxygen when agricultural wastes, called nitrates, help algae to grow and spread so quickly that they use up the light and air that other wildlife needs.

River Pollution and People

When water is polluted by waste, such as sewage, it might end up being used to irrigate fields of crops or for drinking, washing, or cooking. Dirty water like this can carry bacteria and spread infections and disease among people. Dirty water is the main cause of diarrhea, a condition that kills 5,000 children every day according to UNICEF. Waterborne diseases are one of the major causes of death in children under the age of five.

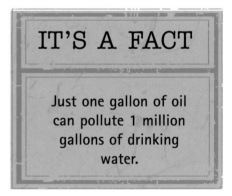

IT'S A FACT

Just one gallon of oil can pollute 1 million gallons of drinking water.

Leachate and Landfill

At poorly managed landfill sites, leachate can pollute land and freshwater supplies. *Leachate* is a toxic liquid produced when rainwater filters through decomposing waste piled in landfills. The better-managed landfill sites solve this problem by sealing the site with a waterproof concrete shell and draining off the leachate. However, some leachate still escapes and in many places, seeps into underground water sources called aquifers. Groundwater is the main source of drinking water for a third of the world's people and it also filters into river resources. Once groundwater is contaminated, it is extremely expensive and difficult, and sometimes impossible, to clean it up.

Evidence

WASTE AND WATER POLLUTION

This diagram shows the different forms of waste that pollute surface and groundwater sources. From fertilizers that filter into soil, to leachate from landfill, sources of fresh water that have taken billions of years to build up above and below ground are under threat from waste pollution.

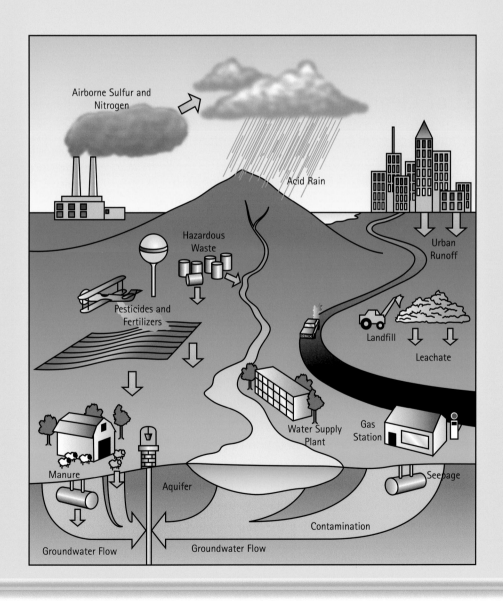

Airborne Sulfur and Nitrogen

Acid Rain

Hazardous Waste

Urban Runoff

Pesticides and Fertilizers

Landfill

Leachate

Water Supply Plant

Gas Station

Manure

Aquifer

Seepage

Contamination

Groundwater Flow

Groundwater Flow

The Cost of Cleaning Up Waste

Waste collection and disposal services provide important work and income for many people around the world, but the cost of cleaning up waste is huge. For example, it costs European Union (EU) governments up to $115 per household to collect trash from cans. This waste looks ugly, smells bad, and attracts disease-carrying pests, such as rats. There is the cost of healthcare for people affected by waste pollution, including cancer patients living near waste disposal sites, who say their condition is caused by dioxins released into the air by waste incineration. Some people argue that the money spent on, or because of, waste could be put to much better use.

As well as the cost of cleaning up everyday pollution, it also costs money to clean up waste from disasters such as oil spills, river pollution, and factories or power stations when they are closed. For example, to clean up the nuclear waste and the land contaminated by a single nuclear power station costs up to $200 billion. Cleaning up oil and oil spills is expensive, because oil spreads out quickly and it does not dissolve in water. It is usually removed by spraying chemicals on it to break it up and by being removed by recovery ships. When an oil tanker called the *Sea Empress* ran aground off Wales in 1996, it released over 72,000 tons of oil into the sea. This cost over $46 million to clean up.

▲ The specialized work of cleaning up seawater, coastal land, and oil-affected wildlife such as seabirds, is enormously expensive.

CASE STUDY
Chewing Gum Waste

Chewing gum is particularly expensive to clean up—a single piece of gum that cost about 6 cents to buy, costs up to $3 to clean up. Chewing gum does not biodegrade, because it is made partly from the same rubber as car tires, so it stays in the environment for a long time. It is so sticky that to remove it from streets, high-pressure water sprays, chemicals, and steam have to be used. These methods can damage sidewalks and the environment, and they are very expensive because they require large amounts of electrical energy. Cleaning up chewing gum waste is such a big issue that in 1992, the government of Singapore, where gum had even stopped electric doors on trains working when it had been left there, passed a law to stop people buying, selling, or using chewing gum at all.

▼ Sorting through waste in places such as Manila, Philippines, provides work for poor people but exposes workers to a range of health hazards.

Wasting Resources

Many of the products that people buy are important to their lives and keep them healthy, comfortable, and happy. However, when people throw away a product, they are also effectively throwing away the natural resources and the energy that have been used to make it. For example, huge quantities of crude oil are used to make plastic items, from toy dolls to cell phones. Resources that are mined from rocks called ores are used to make a huge variety of goods from televisions and tin cans, to cars and computers. Even food that could be eaten is wasted—it is estimated that almost half of the food grown and harvested for consumption in the United States is wasted.

Energy Resources

It takes large amounts of energy to get the raw materials to make products, and even more energy to convert them into goods in factories and to transport them around the world. The production of plastic is similarly energy-intensive. Energy is used to extract the oil that is used to make plastic, and to shape and mold that plastic into a product. Then, if the product runs on electricity, such as an electric toothbrush, it continues using energy throughout its life.

▼ With increasing numbers of people on the planet needing places to live, land is a vitally important resource. One of the resources that waste uses up is land. Waste takes up land for landfill and other waste disposal sites, and land is also effectively wasted when it is used for growing food that just gets thrown away.

Nonrenewable Resources

Some resources are renewable. For example, some of the forests cut for timber can be replanted to provide more wood. However, many of the resources that are used to make products that are then discarded are nonrenewable, including metals, minerals, and oil. There is a limited amount of these resources and one day they will run out. For example, 65 percent of the world's energy is derived from oil or natural gas. These are fossil fuels that formed from organisms that died millions of years ago. At current rates of usage, some scientists predict that gas will run out in less than 60 years and oil in about 40 years.

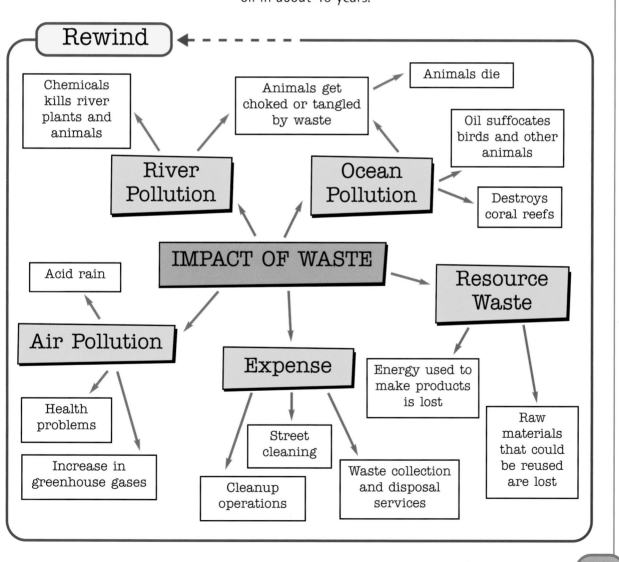

Rewind

Chemicals kills river plants and animals

Animals get choked or tangled by waste

Animals die

Oil suffocates birds and other animals

River Pollution

Ocean Pollution

Destroys coral reefs

Acid rain

IMPACT OF WASTE

Resource Waste

Air Pollution

Expense

Energy used to make products is lost

Health problems

Increase in greenhouse gases

Street cleaning

Cleanup operations

Waste collection and disposal services

Raw materials that could be reused are lost

Sustainable Solutions

Sustainable living means living in a way that does not have a significant negative impact on the environment or other people, and that does not deplete resources for future generations. In order to solve the waste problem, many people are already following the three Rs—reduce, reuse, and recycle. The best way for people to reduce waste is to avoid making it in the first place, by cutting down on the amount of things they use and buy. The next best strategy is to reuse existing products whenever it is possible, and finally, it is also good to recycle, to use materials from a waste product to make something new.

Reducing Waste

There are a number of ways to reduce the amount of waste produced. The simplest way to start is by thinking whether a product is really needed before it is bought. When people shop, they should try to choose products that have little or no packaging and take their own reusable shopping bags rather than using a lot of plastic or paper bags. People can also reduce waste by buying hard-wearing goods that will last longer before they need to be replaced, and goods with parts that can be repaired when they wear out. People can also help by choosing services instead of products, for example renting tools, DVDs, books, and special outfits instead of buying new ones.

► People can often buy food with less packaging at markets, especially farmers' markets, where locally grown produce is sold.

Reducing Energy Use

Individuals can reduce the amount of fuel and electricity they use in various ways—for example, by turning the heating down and installing energy-saving light bulbs at home, and by taking the bus or cycling instead of traveling by car. Buying locally grown food also helps because it reduces the amount of fuel used to transport food around the world. Renewable forms of energy from natural sources, such as the Sun, moving air, or moving water, are also more sustainable because they generate power without depleting nonrenewable resources, such as coal and gas, and they produce very little pollution or greenhouse gases such as carbon dioxide.

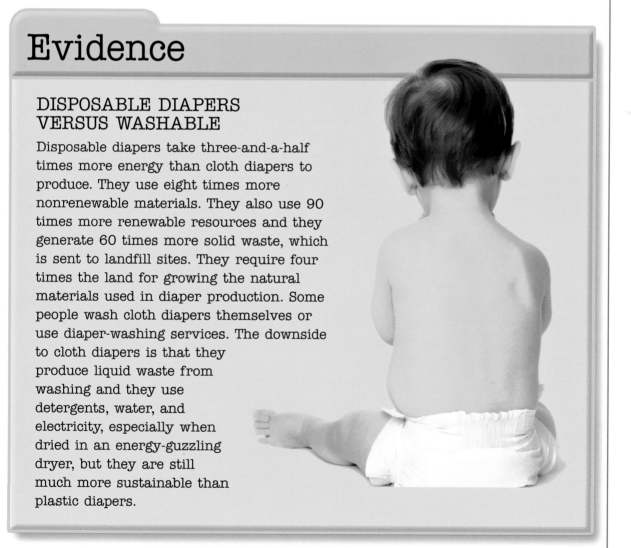

Evidence

DISPOSABLE DIAPERS VERSUS WASHABLE

Disposable diapers take three-and-a-half times more energy than cloth diapers to produce. They use eight times more nonrenewable materials. They also use 90 times more renewable resources and they generate 60 times more solid waste, which is sent to landfill sites. They require four times the land for growing the natural materials used in diaper production. Some people wash cloth diapers themselves or use diaper-washing services. The downside to cloth diapers is that they produce liquid waste from washing and they use detergents, water, and electricity, especially when dried in an energy-guzzling dryer, but they are still much more sustainable than plastic diapers.

Reuse

To reuse something is to clean or repair it and then make use of it again. When a product is reused again and again, this reduces energy use, because no energy is being used to make a new one to replace it, and it saves the cost and environmental damage caused by waste disposal. Reusing something can be as simple and as cheap as printing on both sides of a sheet of paper, or it can be more complex, such as repairing a car or re-covering an old sofa so it can be used again. Reuse also saves money.

Designed for Reuse

Some products are designed to be reused again and again, such as milk bottles or lunchboxes. In some countries, such as Malawi, all bottled drinks are sold on the basis that they can be refilled. If the empty bottle is returned, then a small deposit is returned, encouraging people to reuse bottles. The only downside to this kind of reuse is that an item needs to be returned to the supplier to be washed or treated in some way, to check that it is still fit to be used for its original purpose. This uses up energy and some resources, but is still more preferable to throwing items away and buying new.

IT'S A FACT

Glass milk bottles can be washed and used up to 20 times.

◄ In India, lunch is delivered to workers in metal tiffins. The tiffins are washed and reused each day.

Pass It On!

Things that people no longer need or want, such as old clothes or furniture, can often be passed on to someone who does. Old clothes, shoes, and household linens can be put into clothing collection banks so that they can be sold to people through charity shops, or sent to LEDCs, where they can be used again. Eyeglasses in good condition can also be collected and sent via charities to be reused by people in LEDCs who need them. Computers can be refurbished, repaired, and reused elsewhere, for example, in African schools.

Evidence

REUSING IDEAS

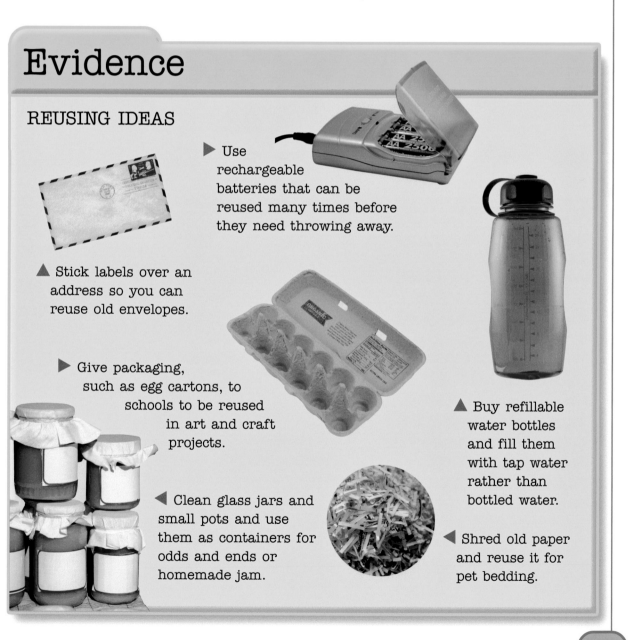

▶ Use rechargeable batteries that can be reused many times before they need throwing away.

▲ Stick labels over an address so you can reuse old envelopes.

▶ Give packaging, such as egg cartons, to schools to be reused in art and craft projects.

◀ Clean glass jars and small pots and use them as containers for odds and ends or homemade jam.

▲ Buy refillable water bottles and fill them with tap water rather than bottled water.

◀ Shred old paper and reuse it for pet bedding.

Recycling by Composting

Recycling turns waste material into raw material for making new products or new forms of energy. One of the simplest forms of recycling is composting. To make compost, organic waste is put into a container or hole in the ground and allowed to decompose, or rot. This process is *aerobic*, meaning organisms such as bacteria and fungi use oxygen as they break down the waste. Compost is a natural fertilizer that enriches soil when it is spread on fields or gardens, and it also restricts weed growth. Composting organic waste reduces waste in landfills and cuts down on the leachate in those sites. Domestic, small-scale composting has been common globally for centuries. Larger-scale collection of food waste by regional government for composting as a solution to food in landfill is more recent. The problem with this is that refuse vans have to collect the waste and this creates traffic and air pollution, so a better solution may be for people to compost their own organic waste.

▲ Recycling for compost treats food waste as a resource instead of rubbish.

IT'S A FACT

In a process that uses heat and pressure, animal waste, such as pig manure, can be turned into liquid fuel to power vehicles.

Recycling Waste into Energy

Waste contains a surprising amount of energy—about one-quarter of the energy of the same weight of coal—and so it can also be recycled to make electricity. As waste at a landfill site rots, it releases methane. This can be collected by drilling holes into the landfills or through underground pipes. The gas is then pumped to an engine, where it is burned to release energy that turns a wheel. The wheel operates a generator that creates electricity. The electricity travels along cables to homes and businesses. Many incinerators create electricity, too, but during this process, they release up to one-third more carbon dioxide than some gas-fired power stations.

Evidence

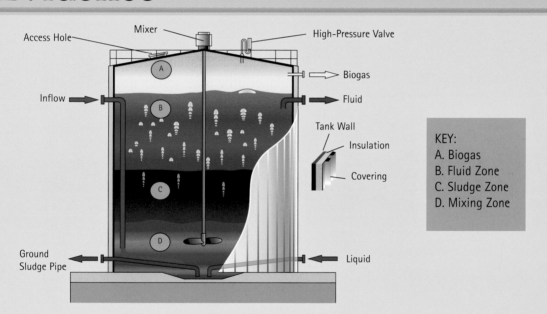

Access Hole
Mixer
High-Pressure Valve
Biogas
Inflow
Fluid
Tank Wall
Insulation
Covering
Ground
Sludge Pipe
Liquid

KEY:
A. Biogas
B. Fluid Zone
C. Sludge Zone
D. Mixing Zone

ANAEROBIC DIGESTION

Anaerobic digestion is a waste-into-energy technology. In an anaerobic digester, waste is crunched up and mixed with liquid to make sludge. This is pumped into a sealed tank that is warm inside. The temperature makes bacteria in the tank thrive. The bacteria break down the waste. They convert part of the waste into biogas, which is a mixture of methane and carbon dioxide. Biogas flows from the tank to power stations to make electricity. Using the gas prevents it from escaping into the atmosphere where it contributes to global warming. The fluid and sludge remaining after bacteria have broken down the waste are pumped out for use, mostly as fertilizer for farms.

What Can be Recycled?

Recycling old products into new involves breaking them down into materials that are then reformed into new objects. Paper, glass, aluminum cans, plastic water bottles, and many other kinds of things can be recycled and turned into a variety of things. Recycled paper is used to make more paper or cardboard. Recycled glass makes new bottles and jars, but it is also used as road-laying material, roof tiles, and fiberglass. Recycled plastic can be turned into trash-can liners and shopping bags, drainpipes, window frames, CD cases, furniture, and clothes, such as waterproof jackets and fleeces. Recycling can also be a quick process. Used cans can be back on the shelves as new cans within six to eight weeks, and it can take just seven days to recycle old newspapers and magazines into new ones.

How Recycling Works

Some countries have schemes that encourage households to sort their types of waste into separate containers to make recycling easier. The separated waste is then collected and taken to recycling sites where it is checked and then melted, or otherwise broken down, in preparation for being reformed into a new product.

Evidence

RECYCLING GLASS

Waste glass is easy to recycle into new bottles or jars.

1 Waste glass is emptied from bottle banks or kerbside collections systems and taken to recycling sites.

2 The glass is crushed and mixed with soda ash and limestone.

3 The mixture is heated in a furnace to about 2,696 degrees Fahrenheit (1,480 degrees Celsius) until it melts into liquid.

4 The melted glass mixture is pressed and blown into molds to form new glass products.

Tricky to Recycle

Some products are easier to recycle than others. Products that are made from a mixture of materials and parts have to be separated before they can be recycled, which is time-consuming and expensive. Taking apart cell phones to recover their tiny components is not worth the effort, and so most are simply thrown away. However, new methods of recycling are being found. For example, new e-waste recycling plants have special technology for separating plastics. Some European countries have reverse vending machines (RVMs). These take and sort different used beverage containers using a laser scanner, which reads codes in the plastic. The RVMs then return money to the person who recycled the container in the machine.

▲ It takes 50 one-quart bottles to make one recycled fleece jacket.

▶ Mount Everest was once known as the highest garbage pile on Earth, because of the waste left there by tourists and climbers. Now, the Nepalese government reduces waste by making expeditions pay a deposit, which is returned if they bring their trash back down with them. Visitors are encouraged to use metal containers, which can be brought down in crushed form, and then recycled and turned into cooking pans and utensils.

▲ Out of sight out of mind? If people had to deal with their own waste, rather than send it abroad, would they create less?

CASE STUDY
The Story of Recycled Plastic Bags

Most of the plastic bags that people in North America and the United Kingdom are given free in stores are made in China, and that is where they go to be recycled. Container ships deliver export products, such as toys, shoes, and MP3 players and plastic bags, and then carry the waste for recycling back to China on their return journeys.

Recycling in China is a cheap option. Cargo costs are low, because the container ships would otherwise be empty and wages are low in rural China. Many families are willing to make their living sorting, breaking up, chopping, and melting plastic waste, or working in the factories that make new plastic products from the waste. One of the biggest problems with this scheme is that when plastic is recycled, it releases POPs (persistent organic pollutants) that linger in the environment and can damage people's health.

The Advantages of Recycling

There are many positive aspects to recycling. Recycling saves resources and it also reduces the amount of waste that has to be disposed of in landfill or incineration sites. Most recycled products also take less energy to produce. This saves resources, such as fossil fuels, saves money, and also reduces pollution. Recycling also creates jobs. About twice the number of people are involved in recycling aluminum as are employed in new aluminum production.

IT'S A FACT

• Recycling aluminum cans and foil saves 95 percent of the energy required to produce new aluminum.

• Recycling one plastic bottle saves enough energy to power a 60W light bulb for six hours.

Disadvantages of Recycling

Although recycling seems like a good solution, it does have some drawbacks. Recycled goods are often more expensive to buy than new products. This is because there is often more labor or specialized industrial processes involved in making recycled goods. There is also a limit on how many times you can recycle certain materials, for example, paper fibers are damaged each time they are recycled and eventually become useless. Therefore, paper can be recycled only six or seven times. Collecting recyclable wastes and delivering them to recycling sites can vastly increase the distances traveled by waste trucks. This uses up fuel and also creates pollution. If a batch of waste glass, for example, contains materials that should not be there, such as china cups or light bulbs, the whole load is often dumped in the nearest landfill. About one-quarter of all waste put in blue sacks for recycling in Phoenix, Arizona, should not be there. It costs the city almost $1 million each year to sort out the mistake.

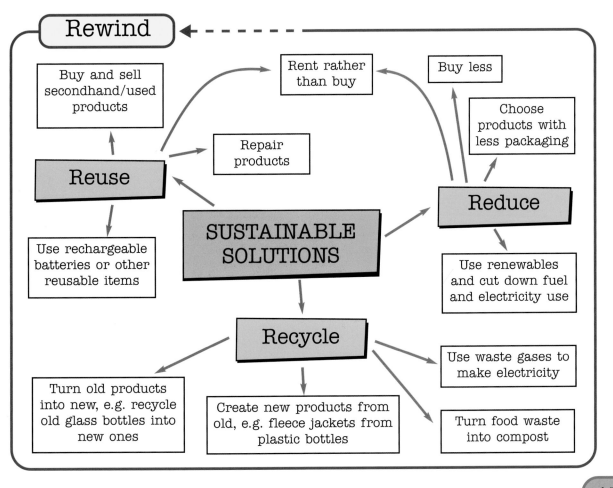

Rewind

Buy and sell secondhand/used products

Rent rather than buy

Buy less

Choose products with less packaging

Repair products

Reuse

Use rechargeable batteries or other reusable items

SUSTAINABLE SOLUTIONS

Reduce

Use renewables and cut down fuel and electricity use

Recycle

Use waste gases to make electricity

Turn old products into new, e.g. recycle old glass bottles into new ones

Create new products from old, e.g. fleece jackets from plastic bottles

Turn food waste into compost

Making Sure the Earth Survives

The global population is increasing all the time. In many parts of the world, the number of factories making new products is also increasing, meaning that more people are also buying more and throwing away more. If people continue generating waste at current rates, by 2050, irreplaceable resources will be lost forever, people will be struggling to find ways of disposing of all the garbage, and the health of the planet and its inhabitants will be harmed.

Planet Under Threat

Waste threatens the future of the planet in a number of ways. When people throw things away, they buy new things to replace them and more of the planet's resources are taken to make the new products. Trees are cut down, mines are dug into the land, and fresh water is depleted. In the future, the pollution caused by today's waste may damage many more rivers and other freshwater sources and drastically reduce the quality of Earth's air supply.

People at Risk

The greenhouse gases released by vehicles and machines as waste and the gases that are emitted by piles of rotting rubbish contribute to climate change. No one really knows what the effects of this will be, but it could mean more dangerous weather events, such as hurricanes and heatwaves, and if temperatures increase and glaciers melt, sea levels will rise and flood low-lying coasts and islands. In the future, fresh water could be in very short supply, and there could be more people suffering from health problems linked to air and water pollution. With fossil fuels running out, people could face regular power cuts, and with space running out, the sight and smell of landfill sites may be much closer to home.

IT'S A FACT

In the future, if everyone in the world lives as wastefully as people in MEDCs do today, the world's population will need the resources of eight planets to survive. There is only one.

Habitat Destruction

When the Earth's resources are overused, wildlife habitats are also destroyed. Most of the world's plant and animal species are under threat today because of habitat destruction. Between 100 and 1,000 species become extinct each year, mainly because the habitats where they live are changing or being destroyed. An *ecosystem* is the plants and animals in a habitat and their environment. Humans rely on ecosystems. Healthy ecosystems help to regulate the planet's climate and provide people with sources of food, water, fresh air, and plant materials that they use for everything from building to making medicines. For ecosystems to work, they need to have a wide variety of species and losing just one of them can change the whole system.

▶ Faced with a bleak future of waste piling up, many places are taking action. Canberra, Australia's national capital, was one of the first cities in the world to adopt a zero waste policy that has reduced the amount of waste going to landfills by almost half in just five years.

A Preferable Future

There are things that people can do to make a difference and achieve a preferable future for the planet. The simplest way to reduce waste is to buy and use less. The waste that is made then needs to be treated as a resource that can be reused or recycled. This will help to conserve resources, reduce pollution, save energy and help the Earth cope with human demands.

Design and Technology

In the future, there could be a drastic reduction in waste if more manufacturers design and produce more durable goods that are more easily taken apart, repaired, reused, or recycled. These will be more expensive to make and buy in the first place, but they will last a lot longer. Money will also be saved because there will be less waste to dispose of. Up until now, technology has been a major cause of waste, but it could also provide solutions. The increasing use of the Internet and email could reduce the need for people to travel so much and reduce the amount of paper used. More goods from renewable materials need to be made, and these should be made using renewable energy resources that can be easily replaced.

Paying for Waste

Governments can provide incentives for industries and individuals to reduce, reuse, and recycle. For example, they could charge people according to the amount of waste they produce. This would encourage people to reduce the amount of waste they make by composting organic waste and recycling more. At the moment, the countries that achieve high recycling rates are those that give financial incentives like this to households to sort out their trash into different categories.

Thinking Globally

A change in the way people think is perhaps the best way toward a preferable future. People need to accept that what they do has an impact on other people and places. The effects might be at a local level, for example, if people make more waste, more landfill sites and incinerators will have to be built near their homes. Or the effects might be global, for example, to make the products people buy, other places may be damaged when mines are dug and trees cut down. The global population's future depends on the health of the environment around the whole planet.

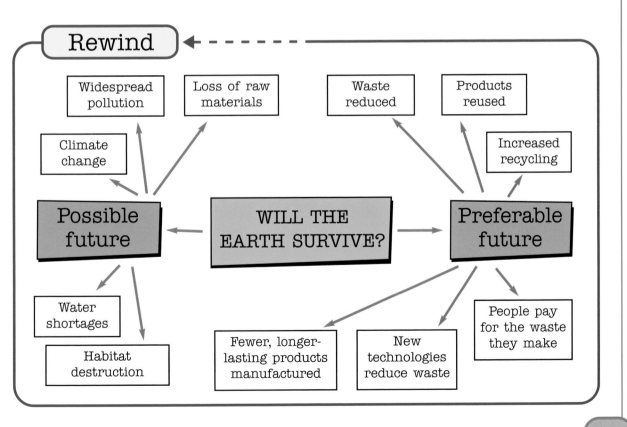

Glossary, Further Information, and Web Sites

Acid rain Rain made acidic by pollutants in the air.

Anaerobic Without oxygen. Aerobic means with oxygen.

Compost The soil-like substance that is formed by the rotting down of organic waste.

Consumer A person who buys or uses a product or service.

Contaminant A substance that pollutes another substance.

Dioxin A poisonous chemical given off when waste is incinerated.

Export To send or transport a commodity abroad for trade or sale.

Fertilizer A substance that helps plants to grow.

Fossil fuels Natural fuels, such as oil, coal, or gas, formed from the remains of things that lived millions of years ago.

Generator A machine that generates, or makes, electricity.

Greenhouse gas A gas in the atmosphere that keeps Earth warm by absorbing the Sun's heat.

Groundwater Water that collects or flows deep underground.

Leachate The black liquid that forms as waste rots.

Methane The gas given off by animal waste. It is one of the greenhouse gases considered responsible for climate change.

Nonrenewable The resources that people use that cannot easily be replaced and that will run out someday.

Ore Solid material, such as rock, from which metal or other minerals can be extracted.

Organic Something that comes from living or once-living things.

Pesticide A substance used to kill pests that eat or damage plants.

Renewable Something that can be replaced so that it does not run out.

Resources Materials from the Earth that people use, such as water, soil, air, trees, and fossil fuels.

Sustainable Describing the careful use of resources, so that they do not run out and we do not damage them for future generations.

Synthetic Artificial, made by people, not found in nature.

Books to read

Cool Science: Recycling
Charlotte Wilcox (Lerner Publications, 2007)

Earth in Danger: Garbage and Recycling
Helen Orme (Bearport Publishing, 2008)

Opposing Viewpoints: Garbage and Recycling
Mitchell Young (Greenhaven Press, 2007)

Your Carbon Footprint series
(Rosen Central, 2008)

Web Sites

Due to the changing nature of Internet links, Rosen Publishing has developed an online list of Web sites related to the subject of this book. This site is regularly updated. Please use this link to access this list:
www.rosenlinks.com/ces/wast

Topic Web

Use this topic web to discover themes and ideas in subjects that are related to waste and recycling.

English and Literacy

• Write a report outlining the steps that could reduce the problem of waste to be read by local and national politicians.

• Debate the pros and cons of charging people according to the amount of waste they produce.

Science and Environment

• Look at environmental problems caused by waste.

• Find out how waste pollution from areas such as Europe travels in air and ocean currents and builds up in Arctic food chains, such as fish, seals, and polar bears.

• Research the difference between acids and alkalis, and which types are hazardous: harmful, irritant, or corrosive substances.

Geography

• Consider the impact of development and how this will affect the quality of life of different people and the amount of waste they produce in the future.

• Look at the patterns of distribution of industries and developments along the River Rhine, and find out about pollutants that enter the river and the effects of this waste.

History and Economics

• Look at waste and sanitation and its effect on life in the Middle Ages.

• Explore the impact of the Industrial Revolution on waste production.

• Explore the different costs of recycling aluminum to make cans and creating new aluminum cans.

Waste and Recyling

Art and Culture

• Picasso recycled trash into artistic treasures. Research some of the art made by Picasso using waste materials.

• Look at photographs of a landfill site, and abstract and simplify the shapes and forms you see to create images that express your ideas about waste and recycling.

• Inspired by the WEEE sculpture on page 11, use waste materials to create a sculpture.

Index